# Will I ever make it, to the awards.

Tyran  Ingram

Presentation by *BookLeaf Publishing*

Web: www.bookleafpub.com

E-mail: info@bookleafpub.com

ISBN: 9789358367775

First edition 2023

*People,places,and things  in your worst days,
still try and be nice. It awards you in your good
days.*

# ACKNOWLEDGEMENT

Thank you to each and every reader, yellow is making history.

# PREFACE

Yellow

# Hello

1

What a day, what a time, things are going good.

# Each time



Umm, I guess I could say the passion is there.

# Waiting

3

Another day of waiting, to think of something to amount to something.

# Can you imagine

Can you imagine, what things could be like, if, you try.

# Yes Yellow

5

If it's nothing new,but it does help people.

# Yes still Yellow

6

Wow, it's nice to be able to see , what Yellow would look like thur sun glasses.lol

# I think you need some yellow

7

Just calm down, and relax it's Yellow though

# An art form of Yellow

8

I think the art form, is the ability to Invision something beautiful, that comes out pure, and thur the pains of life, for a positive outcome.

# Wow

9

So just keep going.

# So, what

The basic, features for Yellow, are the simple things in life.

# Yellow, and paint brushes.

11

Yellow paint can be the imagine you draw.

# The finished Yellow



The painting should come out beautiful, enough to be Yellow.

# Yellow made my day

13

Yellow seemed to make my day honestly.

# Still Yellow

Wow, about half way thru with this book of poems.lol

# Capitalism

15

Add, just add.

# Wow the numbers



If people are in agreement with something they
are passionate about.

# Yellow speaks for itself

17

Yellow, amounted to something.

# Yellow and art portfolio

18

You work in form that others may see

# What should it mean



It could be a lot of words, images, and hashtags, that could represent your work.

# What history would Yellow make

More than just a polite society, but a actually happening or doing, so people can amount to something. Umm but still has faith and religion.

# What I first started on

21

"Add the name of the Lord back to Hollywood." God

Ever now and then people and thoughts, to make do the actual mission. But what leads to a failure in society in too people in your mind, but have everything, but lack a spirit of purity like a kid. A good mood, and mind set for the completion of the mission/hollyness.